Teen Guide to Living With Incarcerated Parents

#TGLWIP

A Self-Help Book for Coping During an Age of Mass Incarceration

For kids like me.

My Mom's Favorite Quote

"It is in the quiet crucible of your personal private sufferings that your noblest dreams are born, and God's greatest gifts are given in compensation for what you've been through."

by Wintley Phipps

[GaitherVEVO]. (2012, April 6). *Bill & Gloria Gaither - It Is Well With My Soul [Live] ft. Wintley Phipps*. [Video File]. Retrieved from https://youtu.be/E8HffdyLd0c.

Table Of Contents

My Champions

"This indispensable work is powerful yet concise, informed by years of experience grappling with the brokenness produced by our criminal justice system's commitment to mass incarceration. It is evidence that love and healing can triumph over hate and harm, if one has the commitment to put in the work."

****

Baz Dreisinger, Ph.D.

Professor, English

Founding Academic Director, Prison-to-College Pipeline

Author, Incarceration Nations: A Journey to Justice in Prisons Around the World (2016)

"Young's work is a testament to both the healing power and deep reservoir of wisdom those who endure the worst of our country's criminal justice system have to offer. The frustrating wonder of this guide -- forged from devastation widely understood as needless and counterproductive -- is that its unquestioned value is only matched by the absurd reality that it had to be written at all."

****

Glenn E. Martin

Founder and President, JustLeadershipUSA

Anyé Young is a Caribbean-American teen model, singer and aspiring actress. She was born in Greensboro, NC (USA) to a Caribbean mother and an American father. Her mother hails from The Nature Island of the Caribbean: The Commonwealth of Dominica.

With confidence and a world class personality, this young author grasps her own destiny firmly in hand as she prepares to cross the cusp of adulthood. She shares her innermost turmoil: her fear of being judged by those who have not walked a mile in her shoes. #TGLWIP is a project encouraged by her mother, Dàna "LaDàna" Drigo, and allows the author a platform to share her truth.

Anyé is currently an 11th grader in high school residing in the Washington, D.C. metro area. *Teen Guide to Living With Incarcerated Parents (#TGLWIP)* is her first book. For more information, visit www.AnyeYoung.com.

Foreword by Gabriel J. Christian, Esq.

#TGLWIP - A Gem Produced by A Role Model

for Civic Duty

In the last quarter of 2015, my wife Joan Christian and I were introduced to LaDàna Drigo and her dynamic daughter, Anyé Young. We met while doing relief work on behalf of Rebuild Dominica Inc, a nonprofit formed to aid our land of birth — The Commonwealth of Dominica — after certain rural areas had been devastated by Tropical Storm Erika. Anyé and her mother impressed us with their sense of civic duty as they presented as loving and compassionate volunteers who always made themselves available to work on fundraising efforts to aid Dominica and other Caribbean islands similarly in need.

When I was told that Anyé had written a book titled "Teen Guide to Living with Incarcerated Parents", I was even more impressed. Why so? Well, I did not know that Anyé Young had survived the trauma attendant to her father being incarcerated. She had shown no deficit in way of grace, compassion, discipline or commitment; characters traits often associated with youngsters bereft of the guiding hands of a parent.

That Ms. Young has done so well in school, community work, and retained a positive outlook on life, is perhaps due to the indomitable spirit of her mother LaDàna Drigo, her grandparents and community. On the other hand, Anyé would not have benefited from such assistance from a single parent where she was not blessed, deep within, with the spirit of wisdom. And it is that spirit of wise effort which has allowed her to transform a negative (the absence of her father) into a positive by publishing this book.

Statistics show that children of the incarcerated are more likely to commit crimes, more likely to fail at school,

more likely to fall prey to unplanned
teenage pregnancy and less likely to
graduate from high school. Mass
incarceration in the United States, born
of racial profiling in an often biased so-
called justice system, has decimated wide
swathes of the African American community.
Other communities of marginalized people
are now suffering from what African
Americans have suffered for decades.

The political class, on the state and
federal level, has done little to craft
public policy to shield the children of
the incarcerated by providing them
services to overcome the absence of their
parents. It is that void left by an often
uncaring society that Anyé Young's book
#TGLWIP hopes to fill.

As a guide, this book lovingly shows the
children of incarcerated parents the way
toward a better future by encouraging them
to aspire to their better selves. #TGLWIP
does not wallow in self-pity, hate or
blame. Rather it encourages our youngsters

afflicted by absent parents to stay in school, study hard, embrace their faith, join youth leadership organizations, volunteer for worthy causes, respect their supportive family circle, and strive for excellence in all things.

For Anyé Young the choice was clear – struggle to overcome the absence of her father or succumb to defeat born of shame and loss. She chose to struggle and win! In doing so Anyé has made a monumental contribution to the betterment of a nation where #TGLWIP shows all of us how we, in the words of Dr. Martin Luther King, Jr., can overcome. I highly recommend this book to all who seek a better day!

~~~

Gabriel J. Christian, Esq. is a Maryland trial lawyer, owner/founder of www.marylandattorneyatlaw.com, and a Caribbean community development activist.

Preface by Anyé's Mother

You are not your parent. I say this to the teens reading this book. And, I say this to my daughter as well. As Anyé's mother, I learned first-hand her frustrations. She shares them with me when we talk about her father's incarceration. And I make it a point to continue to encourage her to talk out her feelings and express herself in a positive manner. I encourage you to also find ways to motivate yourself through those around you.

Remember that each and every day you are blessed to wake up there is a chance for you to continue your mission. This mission could be studying the night before school to ace your next test. Whatever the mission, always look for ways to be productive. Focus your energy on what you CAN change. This is the best advice that I can offer you.

There will be good days and there will be days that you miss being able to hug your mother or father. On those not-so-good days, I encourage you to find someone -- an anchor -- who you trust and feel comfortable enough to talk to about your feelings of hurt and disappointment. This may be your in-house parent, grandparent, an aunt, or an uncle. You may even find good counsel with someone at your local church or a guidance counselor at your school. Whatever you decide to do to get those negative feelings out, please do not internalize your pain.

It will take time to process and understand how to deal with what you are feeling. There will be times along the way when you feel like no one could possibly know what you are going through. On those difficult days, look for inspiration in activities that make you feel happy. Better yet, put your energy into helping others who may be less fortunate than you. It may sound cliché, but this is what Anyé did to overcome the shame she felt.

She took pen to paper and faced her anxiety head-on. She made a conscious decision to share her trials and tribulations with you right here in this book. Writing this guide for teens, like herself, who have an incarcerated parent was a way for her to begin to heal her emotional wounds. In offering this self-help book, Anyé discovered that she was stronger than she gave herself credit.

She also realized that her father being incarcerated was only a negative reflection on her own life if she allowed it to be. Instead of hiding from her truth, she chose to inspire other teens who could benefit from the #TGLWIP -- Teen Guide to Living With Incarcerated Parents.

I don't claim to know exactly how you feel. However, I do know it takes a village to raise a child. I know this from experience in raising my own daughter into the motivated and loving teen she is today.

Anyé transformed the hurt and pain she was feeling from learning that her father couldn't physically be at her side for a decade of her life. She transformed it into #TGLWIP. This is a project of love, inspiration and hope.

Anyé's goal is simple. She wants you to know that you are not alone. She also wants you to remember that you are loved!

~ ~ ~

LaDàna Drigo is a certified public relations professional, a media producer and owner/founder of www.AbovePrestigePR.com. She is a professional speaker who encouraged her daughter, Anyé Young, to use her voice and share her story with the purpose of inspiring both young and old to do the same.

Acknowledgements

I'd like to send a special shout-out to all of the sidewalks for keeping me off the streets. You guys are the real MVPs. But most of all, I thank my Granny, Grandpa, Nana, Chivon (my Godmother) and Nennen (my mom's Godmother) for helping my Mom to raise me for these past years.

Even when they didn't have to, they always made sure I was squared away and had what I needed. They have truly been a blessing and, though they may not have heard it often enough, I do love and appreciate them.

There is another very important person in my life that cannot be forgotten here. They have pushed me to be all that I can be and more. Even at times where I doubted myself, they never gave up on me. They believed in me when I didn't believe in myself. Thank you, Mom.

Introduction

I honestly don't expect pity from anyone.
Mostly because I don't want it and I don't
need it. My Dad is in prison because of
the mistakes he made on his own. I never
told anyone, not even my closest friends,
about what was really going on because I
was embarrassed and ashamed. When people
asked me about my Dad, I didn't lie to
them completely. It would be more like
lying by omission. I would tell them that
my Dad lived in North Carolina, while
excluding the fact that he was actually in
prison.

I was embarrassed because people always
look at parents and compare them to their
children. And, the way I see it, if people
looked at me and knew that my Dad was in
prison, they would think that I was a
criminal in training. Hey, everyone
judges. That judgment is something I
always try to avoid dealing with. I put up

walls between friendships and even my relationship with my mother all because I became uninterested in opening up. Not only that, but I didn't want people's pity. It made me feel like I was weak or inferior, which could only make the situation worse. So, to deal with it, I decided NOT to deal with it. Which is quite contradictory. But allow me to explain…

Chapter 1: My Family

My family can be quite dysfunctional, in my opinion. I've always lived with my Mom, and after my Mom decided to no longer be with my Dad, I saw my Dad's side of the family less often than usual. Several years later, my mother moved to Maryland and so did I.

My family on my Dad's side never really acknowledged me afterwards. They had my phone number… but they never called. I also have three half-brothers and one half-sister… They don't keep in touch either. And, well… that's cool. I'm not close to my Dad's side like I used to be, but I am still close to my Dad. However, I can't say much for my siblings. I know that some of them don't contact him at all, much less even write him a letter. But I do. Just because he basically shot himself in the foot doesn't mean that I have to be insensitive. His situation is

his own fault; yes. But him being in
prison is punishment enough. So, to ignore
him, or to do anything to hurt his
feelings, is pointless. Being angry isn't
really my thing.

When it comes to the subject of incarceration, I've come to realize something about my family: a pattern. My grandfather on my Dad's side was incarcerated… And now, so is his son (my Dad). But it doesn't just stop there because my Dad's son, who is also my oldest half-brother, is now in jail. If that's not a pattern, I don't know what is.

It's like someone in each generation of Black men gets their turn behind bars. They follow in their parent's footsteps making the same terrible decisions and disregarding the fact that they are in turn jeopardizing their own freedom.

When I was overseas, I used to try to talk to my older brother about these things. I made sure to call him at least once a month to make sure he wasn't getting himself in trouble. I still remember seeing his ankle sensor when I was little. When I still lived in North Carolina, he was on probation. I still don't know the full story or the reason why he was under house arrest. He was about 17 or 18

then. That's pretty much how these things
start. I'd talk to him about ending up in jail
and not being able to care for his small
daughter. But, from what I can tell, it all
went in one ear and out the other. Maybe he
never listened to me because I was "just a
kid".

- **Don't expect your family to be perfect**

  Spoiler Alert: <u>no family is perfect</u> so don't expect the dynamic to be anywhere near perfect.

- **Keep in touch**

  Write letters from time to time. Prison is punishment enough

- **Don't be angry over things you can't control**

  Being upset won't change the reality so don't let it affect your mood.

- **Don't hold a grudge**

  They dug a hole for themselves, true. But you can write a letter about how you feel it and MOVE ON. Holding a grudge is <u>useless and unhealthy.</u> Try forgiving them for their mistakes. Probably easier said than done, but, it's worth it.

29

Chapter 2: The Good, The Bad, The Dad

Before being incarcerated, my Dad was a
total gamer and engineer. He was always
into Star Wars; literally his favorite
movie. Every time I went trick-or-treating
when I was younger, he would dress up as
either Yoda or Darth Vader from the Star
Wars movies. He was a pretty devoted fan.

Once my parents separated, my mom moved to
Charlotte, North Carolina. I was 5 1/2
years old at the time. I no longer saw him
every day; just on some weekends. It was
hard not to take sides when they were
angry with each other. At the time, I
didn't know why they were on bad terms.
The first time I started asking questions
about the relationship, I was about 7
years old. I asked him why my Mom was mad
at him. He simply told me that she was
crazy which, if you ask me, was kind of
accurate as far as her overall personality
once you upset her. But it was a bull-crap

answer for this particular question because people don't get angry for no reason.

As I got older, I began to understand that he was cheating on her. And, because my Mom didn't want to put up with it, she ended the relationship and moved from Greensboro to Charlotte (North Carolina). While my Mom and I lived in Charlotte, my Dad came around less and less. A few years later, my mother found out that he had a new child with the woman my mother left him because of. When my Dad knew that she had found out, he stopped providing for me altogether. My mother had to provide for us both by herself for almost a year. Eventually, my mother sent me to live with my grandmother in a French West Indies island. I lived there for almost 3 years until my Mom got back on her feet.

While I was overseas, my mother had gotten a call from my Dad telling her that he was in prison. This wasn't a shock for me because I noticed that his phone was out of service. My Dad never let his phone get cut off. He was sentenced for 12 whole years. Isn't that great! (I hope you detected my delightful sarcasm).

My Dad won't be there for my high school graduation. He'll never be able to see me cheerlead at any of my games. And most of all, he's going to miss a LOT of birthdays. Lots and lots of birthdays…

I hope that he's no longer in prison by the time I go to college in two years. But these are things my Dad will miss out on because of his poor decisions.

My Dad isn't in prison because he killed or kidnapped anyone. He's in prison because he stole. I'll be around 20 years old by the time he gets out. Ever heard of double jeopardy? It's when you are tried twice for the same case and it is prohibited by law.

The way my Dad explained it to me, he was actually tried twice for a case where he was previously found innocent. Nevertheless, his sentence is pretty lengthy for a theft crime. His total sentence is about 12 years and 3 months. And by the time his term is up, I'll be finishing up college.

Imagine never ever being able to get that time back. Imagine remembering your kid as a 9-year-old and by the time your term is up, they're already a full-fledged adult in college.

- **Remember the good times**

  Focusing on the bad memories will only make you hate your incarcerated parent. So, acknowledge the good things about that person to keep positive.

- **Accept the reality**

  That person will probably miss out on some things you wish they were there to witness. But you can't change that. You have to learn to cope with reality.

- **Appreciate what you DO have**

  When you look at other families that seem to have it all together, don't let it fool you. Don't focus on what you don't have… Instead, embrace what you do have.

- **Know that it is not the end of the world**

  That person is no longer with you, sure. But life goes on. At some point you have to learn to continue living your life instead of constantly occupying your mind with **unnecessary** and **stressful** thoughts.

Chapter 3: Mommy Dearest

My mother is very caring and loving. She has ambition, which I get from her. She's one of those people who wants more out of life than getting a good job, getting married and having kids. But like any other mother, she's not perfect. This was something that I needed to understand. Taking care of a child all on your own isn't easy; especially when they're a teenager. Teenagers are trying to figure themselves out and it doesn't help that we have to worry about homework, tests, and college for that matter.

Eventually, I developed anxiety and clashing at home with my mother did no good. Deep down, I was upset towards my Dad and little disputes with my Mom would cause me to overreact. However, it takes two to tango. Again, my Mom isn't perfect. Then again, who is?

Until recently, I felt that my Mom never really understood me. So, therefore, when she made assumptions without really letting me explain myself, she often missed out on information. After some time, I gave up because I felt like she didn't want to hear me out. I felt like my Mom didn't completely know me. At the same time, you shouldn't expect a 14-year-old to still act like a 9-year-old.

Personalities change. My Dad going to prison kind of made me care a little less about things. I would just let everything pass by. Avoiding stress was what I was essentially trying to do. But of course, no one would be able to understand that besides me unless I told them. And I wasn't the type of person to talk about my problems or my feelings.

My Mom hated this about me. But she didn't understand that not talking about it actually helped me. I often kept to myself when it came to how I felt. I was wrong

for not opening up, but, I felt
uncomfortable not having my Dad around.
Especially, when she would take me to do
things that I usually did with my Dad.
Like going to Dave & Buster's, for
example. Before my Dad went to prison,
Dave & Buster's was our thing. So, going
there without him was a sore reminder of
the fact that he was not around.

My Mom has always been the independent type of woman. But, some things aren't meant to be done alone. Raising a child would be one example.

I know what it's like to see your peers at parent/teacher conferences and they have both of their parents by their side, whilst you only have one. My Mom had to go as far as sending me overseas to live with my grandmother for almost three years because she couldn't bare having to make me struggle with her. When she finally moved from North Carolina to Maryland, she was living with her college friend and her godmother. After saving up for a few months, she got her first apartment.

And, even then, it was two years after she got her own place that she was able to have me come back stateside. And boy, was I happy to be back!

While I lived in Guadeloupe, a French Caribbean island, the children that were there weren't all that welcoming. Especially since I was American. They practically hated me for being an American citizen and it only got worse the longer I stayed there. Being back in the U.S. has definitely relieved me of the verbal abuse from students in Guadeloupe. There's still the occasional "beef" here. But…. that's just high school. So, it's pretty much inevitable.

One thing I will say is my Mom has always been there to guide and provide for me. She's all I have. I can only imagine how many sacrifices she has to make to make sure that I get what I need. She didn't make me alone. Yet, she has to do everything on her own. My Dad couldn't do his part as a father because he was too selfish to consider what I, as his child, would have to go through if he ended up in prison. He's the one who made that mistake. Yet, my mother is the one who has to pay.

- **Don't push people away**

  Yeah, they probably don't understand your point of view. But don't punish them for it.

- **Try to get along with the person taking care of you**

  This is the only person who cares enough to make you their responsibility. So, don't take them for granted or damage the relationship.

- **Cut a little slack**

  Whomever is taking care of you, give them a break sometimes. Ultimately, there is no tutorial on how to deal with a teenager. So, understand that they may just be doing their best.

- **Pull, not push**

  If you're very upset, don't pass it out on the people around you. You'll make them distance themselves. And that helps no one.

Chapter 4: Aspirations and Goals

My current goal, as far as education is concerned, is to maintain good grades in school; especially my GPA. This isn't always an easy task when you're constantly thinking about someone in your life, who had been there, not being by your side. The way I dealt with this was by not thinking about the negative side... at all.

When do I have to start thinking about my future? Well, ... now! Not only is my goal to graduate high school with a very high GPA, but I am also working on my certification in Video Production. And I learn as much as I can with my Theatre classes. I will graduate high school because my Dad didn't. I will also attend and graduate from college to prove that, in spite of my challenges, I can be a beacon of hope for other children like me. I am using my situation to turn this

challenging time into exciting milestones.
I want to succeed where my Dad failed.

In the very near future, I want to become
a working actress. The situation my Dad is
in gives me even more ambition and more
reasons to pursue my goals. Instead of
looking at the negatives, focus on the
positives. You just need to find the
silver lining. Basically, I refuse to let
my Dad's failures have any negative effect
on my success.

I've been into acting since I was little. Shows from Nickelodeon and Disney Channel really inspired me to want to act in movies and cool shows I'd enjoyed watching. I did my first ever play in 8th grade. I was cast as Tzeitel in *Fiddler on the Roof (Junior)*. But it really wasn't until I began to take Film Production classes in high school that I started to consider the different roles one could take.

Taking video production classes wasn't even my idea. I thought it sounded boring. My Mom is the one who practically forced me to take the class and I ended up falling in love with everything about it. The idea that one could change so much about a story through editing is amazing to me. I learned to use camera angles, frames, and camera movements to set a specific tone or mood. I also loved that I could explore the components that to go into movie-making. It was then that I knew that I wanted to do more than just be in movies.

I wanted to be able to make my own movies too.
I feel like the reason I'm so passionate about
these things is because most of my family on
my Dad's side didn't make it to college. I
don't want that to be my case. It's the reason
I work so hard for excellent grades. It's the
reason I make sure that I am competitive.
Because when it comes down to it, getting
admitted into college is a competition --- and
I refuse to settle!

I refuse to be like my Dad and settle for only
a G.E.D. I refuse to live a mediocre life. I
want more than the bare minimum. I want to be
better than that. I'd like to be able to
afford whatever I want and enjoy the finer
things in life because I know that with all
that I've gone through, I deserve it.

- **Set your own goals**

  Don't let your situation have any effect over your aspirations in life.

- **Get involved**

  Instead of alienating yourself, make friends, join sports teams or clubs. Take your mind off the negative things.

- **Do things that make you happy**

  No one likes to be unhappy. It's not fun! But guess what? Doing things that make you happy, will make you happy... Crazy concept, right?

- **Set yourself up**

  Start thinking about your future **NOW!** Preparation is always a good thing. You won't be young forever. Unless, you're me.

Chapter 5: Eventually

My goal when I grow up is to be a working actress. I also want to direct movies and produce television shows. I'm setting myself up now, even though I am only 15, to be successful in the future. It's always good to know your strengths so you can plan ahead, … WAY ahead.

I've encountered people that don't know what they want to do in the future and settle for the first job they can get. Well, I wouldn't want that for myself. I want to be one of those people who wake up and don't mind going to work because they like their job. Instead, I intend to go to work because I love doing what I do EVERY day. Who wouldn't want to get paid for doing something they love doing?

I don't want to become an adult who can't stand their job and can't wait to go home or who live paycheck to paycheck. And, to be honest, I'm not thinking about having kids when I get older. I can barely keep up with myself. However, if I do decide to become a parent one day and have a kid, I would teach him or her to have ambition and to get what they want out of life because that's what I'm doing.

School is something I take very seriously. When I get anything low like a C or B, the depression just rolls in. I know I'm never going to be the perfect student, but I can still try. I already have a 4.0 GPA, but I make sure I never slack off.

Apart from my grades, I'm in a few clubs; like Forensics which gives me acting performance practice during the school year. And other things like cheerleading, which I only do in the fall so I can do theatre productions in the winter season.

By the end of my sophomore year in high school, I got straight A's. Because of these good grades, I started to get emails from universities left and right. They are trying so desperately to recruit me as a student. Everything seemed to be going great. That is until cheer tryouts last August.

I ended up not making the Varsity team and my soul was crushed. After that, I wasn't myself for days because I was so heartbroken. Then I

realized that there's always basketball season
and in order to keep myself occupied during
the fall, I could simply do another theatre
production. After all, cheerleading isn't
going to get me anywhere in life. I am not
planning on being a professional cheerleader
for any national team.

I realized then that my priorities weren't
straight. I should have been worrying more
about something that is going to help my
career in the future rather than worrying
about something that isn't. When I did not
make the fall varsity cheer team, I realized
this just gave me more time to focus on
theatre.

- **Focus on your future**

  There are some things that you can't change, yes. However, there are some things that you actually have power over. How you live your life being one of them. You have the ability to steer the wheel and make good decisions.

- **Know what you want**

  What do you want out of life? That's for you to decide. Don't allow yourself to get lost in the real world, **know what you want.**

- **Have a social life**

  Of course, education is very important and should always come first. But having a couple of friends wouldn't hurt. Get out of the house every now and then when you have free time.

- **Don't make the same mistakes**

  Seeing other people's harsh consequences for their poor decisions

51

should motivate you to not follow in
their footsteps.